Cultural Genocide
and the
Italian-American Legacy

A Culture Hijacked by Popular Myth
and
Media Misrepresentation

SEVERINA MARINETTI

CULTURAL GENOCIDE AND THE
ITALIAN–AMERICAN LEGACY
A CULTURE HIJACKED BY POPULAR MYTH
AND MEDIA MISREPRESENTATION

iUniverse books may be ordered through booksellers or by contacting:

iUniverse
1663 Liberty Drive
Bloomington, IN 47403
www.iuniverse.com
1-800-Authors (1-800-288-4677)

ISBN: 978-1-4917-9146-2 (sc)
ISBN: 978-1-4917-9147-9 (e)

Print information available on the last page.

iUniverse rev. date: 07/20/2016

From the Renaissance to the radio and from two millennia prior and several centuries preceding, the majestic country of Italy and its visionary people have taken the world "by storm". The influence that this richly diverse little peninsula has had in the sciences, arts and in every other field and discipline continue to resonate throughout the planet. Multitudes of Italian inspired accomplishments continue to wow the nations, on a regular basis. However, in America, a pervasive denial of the intellect and sophistication of the Italian people and culture only seems to be intensifying in this age in which so many consider themselves to be "culturally sensitive" and "politically correct". This specific strain of bigotry is a homegrown plague and is not prevalent in most other countries of the world. (Yet, the presence of American movies and television in these places does pose a threat). I have held conversation with many Italian-Americans who, like myself, have felt bewildered as to how distorted our collective image has become. The repulsive stock characterization of the "typical" Italian-American which is far too frequently held as the prototype could not be further from the reality of the "paisani" whom I have known in my lifetime. I believe that we Italian-Americans have, as a group, fallen into a "perfect storm" which has dismembered our reputation as a class five hurricane or a tidal wave would tear apart and pulverize the individual parts of a ship. As in a "perfect storm" several factors work together to sink a ship, we have fallen prey to more than a handful of disadvantages as well as carefully orchestrated schemes which have all contributed to the widely accepted defamation of one of the most amazing groups of people and cultures in the world.

AS A SWEEPING GENERALIZATION, WE ITALIAN-AMERICANS HAVE CONSISTENTLY BEEN IN THE RIGHT PLACE AT THE WRONG TIME ON THIS CONTINENT.

The greatest number of Italians arrived in America in the late nineteenth and early twentieth centuries. They sailed into New York Harbor just in time to be swept off to work in the sweat shops and coal mines, or to fight in the First World War. At this time, labor unions were virtually non-existent, working conditions were treacherous, pay was low and discrimination was legal and thriving. The second generation, of stateside Italians who were the children of these poor laborers, "enjoyed" much of the same disprivilege. They inherited the social status of the underclassman. They held the worst jobs, suffered from prejudice and were, as it happened, shipped off to fight their own world war, as well. (I will elaborate on the Italian-Americans of the "greatest generation", later on).

At the time most of our forefathers arrived in the New World, people were categorized as Black, White and Oriental. The "Red" man was unfortunately no longer a prominent part of the picture and Hispanics were more or less concentrated in the Southwest. This put the Italian immigrant in an ambiguous situation. In fact, I would venture to say that if ever there were a "Gray" man, it was then and still is the Italian-American. As it was, we were deemed legally "White" just as the Irish, German, and Eastern European immigrants who were also trudging through Ellis Island in mass. Yet, our Anglo-Saxon host culture did not view us as White by any stretch of the imagination. In addition to many other inhospitable acts, which will be discussed shortly, we were encouraged, if not forced to do one thing above all else: BE AMERICAN!

It has always been my opinion that the direct translation of this command actually means, "BE ENGLISH!" We were instructed to abandon our mother tongue and culture altogether. We were supposed to speak English and ONLY English. We were to reject the practice of La Befana, leaving gifts for our children on the Epiphany, and begin putting our Santa gifts out on Christmas morning. Even our names were changed. In my own family, my father "Geno" was baptized "Eugene" My grandfather "Giovanni" became "Johnny"; the list goes on. I went to high school with many an Italian-American granddaughter of these immigrants who, for example, sported surnames such as "Ross" and "Perry", instead of "Rossi" and "Perino". The verbal butchers employed at Ellis Island were not the only guilty parties. It was a common practice of the time for parents to anglicize their surnames and their children's first names. They believed they were acting in their families' best interests by doing so, and may have been, in the short term.

I once heard an interview with actor/director Penny Marshall in which she divulged that she did not even know when she was growing up that her family was Italian. It was kept a secret as if it were some wretched skeleton in the closet. She said she grew suspicious because her father discretely ate a lot of pasta. I cannot even fathom the severity of the harm that this practice could have on a young person's self-image. We have all heard the heartbreaking stories of fairly completed Black people "passing" as White and the psychological and familial harm that this practice caused. What happens then if entire families deny their heritage? I am sure the practice was more widely spread amongst Italians, given that they have European features to begin with. Incidentally, shortly after directing the major motion picture "Big", the film grossed $100,000,000. This earned her the distinction of being the first female director in the world to hit this number. Because of her anglicized name, not many people see this as one of "our" accomplishments, nor does some Italian-American girl who dreams of becoming a Hollywood director gain the role model.

Again, parents like the "Marshalls" as well as the millions of Italian-Americans who thought they were acting in their children's best interest by not teaching them the language and by "anglicizing everything up" as much as possible, thought they were protecting their children from the harsh treatment they would otherwise receive as Italian-Americans. This threat did and still does exist. Though my last name ends in a vowel, it is only two syllables long and is not immediately recognized by many non-Italians as an Italian name. Upon meeting people, I have frequently been asked, "What kind of a name is that?" I have personally experienced disapproval on many occasions upon boldly responding, "It's Italian".

When I sense a negative reception, I usually ask the disapprover what his or her ethnicity is. They often beam with pride when they tell me, "I am Irish," "I am Bohemian and French", etc., as if they have beaten me at something. There are others who insist, "I am American!", as if I have to pick one side of the fence and cannot be Italian-American. (As a general rule, I have found Italian-Americans to be very patriotic).

I like to inform these "patriots" that I am as American as they come. My grandfather fought in WWI and my father and all of my uncles fought in WWII. Because I celebrate the feast of Saint Joseph and eat fish on Christmas Eve instead of turkey does not make me less American than those who tell me to behave more like an American. It makes me less English. I have asked a couple of these more aggressive "Americans" over the years if they hunt bison and live on a reservation. I have also never met one that participated in a powwow, except on the sidelines with a camera and a tour bus waiting to take him/her back to the hotel. Most of you reading this probably grew up celebrating Thanksgiving with gusto, but start the meal with a pasta course before the turkey. My point is, there are many different ways to be American and this being the "land of the free", no individual needs to give up their heritage in order to do so.

Over the years, our racial identity has taken several spins on the color wheel, but it never seems to stop for long. I can personally remember as far back as the 1970's. At this time, Hispanics and Italians were, generally, viewed to be far more similar than we are now. We are all predominantly Catholic, generally darker in pigment than Anglo-Saxons and speak a language other than English which is derived from the ancient Latin. I can remember in my youth, people asking me, "Are you Hispanic or Italian?"

As previously stated, the racial "slots" in which human beings are placed frequently change. By the 1970's, it was still believed that there were only three races. At this point they were: Negroid, Caucasoid and Mongoloid. Obviously Negroid refers to Black people and Caucasoid to White. Mongoloid included not only Asian people, but also Aboriginals and American Indian. Hence, the groundwork was laid for Hispanics to call themselves "non-White', since most Latin-Americans have both Spanish and "West Indian blood". At this point in time, it was becoming more advantageous to be deemed non-White. The Civil Rights Amendment had passed and affirmative action laws were on the table. Legal recourse for victims of racial discrimination in housing, education and employment became an option as affirmative action made newer public housing and scholarships more available to legally recognized minorities. Thus, Hispanics lobbied for the rights to be recognized as a unique race. As you know, this was granted; and after several years of calling themselves "Hispanic", they decided to instead call themselves, "Latino". The argument was that "Hispania" is not an actual place, (even though Hispaniola and Latin America are actual locations). Therefore, one term was deemed more accurate than the other.

This has been a reoccurring blow to our heritage. In order to satisfy other ethnic groups, we Italian-Americans have often been given the "short end of the stick". The argument that "Latin America is a place and Spanish is a romance language is a perfect example. Latin America is an actual place, absolutely. What about Rome? That "actual place" is in the actual country of Italy and is the "actual" center of the former Roman Empire as well as the birthplace of the "actual" Latin language. As far as Spanish being a Latin language, it is; but Italian is Latin's only direct descendent. After all, look again at where it is spoken. Any linguist will assure you that Italian is the closest living language to Latin. Latin-American literature often substitutes the term "Anglo" for Caucasian. I have a problem with this. Italians, who can frequently trace their heritage back to Ancient Rome cannot refer to themselves as "Latin" and now are lumped into the category of "Anglo" by the very people who hijacked the title "Latin". If this is not racial insensitivity, I do not know what is. I continue to refer to writers from Latin America as Hispanic or Latin American. I will not refer to them as Latino until I am permitted to refer to myself as Latina, as well. I am not being insensitive, I am being consistent. I also continue to use the term Black for those of African descent instead of African-American. When the term White is abandoned for European-Americans, I will change this practice, as well. Inconsistent treatment of people based on their origin is a form of racism. Therefore, I will not practice this form of inconsistency.

I have a neighbor who is from Argentina. Her primary language is, of course Spanish, but she has two Italian grandparents and two German grandparents. She is able to claim her race to be "Latino" not because of her actual Roman heritage, but because Argentina is a Spanish-speaking country. She does so because she enjoys "minority benefits", as she says. I have known many blonde haired and blue eyed people from Spain who do the same. Yet again, Italians are not legally allowed to partake in this. By this token, I think that French, Portuguese and Romanians should be able to check the "Latino" box wherever they could benefit from doing so. After all, these are also Romance languages.

It seems that once again, the winds of cultural sensitivity have blown over us. Although I would not wish to tackle the repulsive task of putting human beings into such categories, I must argue that Italians, Greeks, Spaniards and other Mediterranean people should be given a race of their own, as have Hispanics, Arabs, etc.

On those "check your race" sections of forms which we complete at the DMV or on any number of other occasions, I always check "other". Perhaps this is a relatively unproductive gesture. Yet, it leaves me with a small sense of satisfaction. In some way, I feel as if I am taking a "baby step" away from the assimilation which was forced upon us.

In addition to being able to check a unique race, Hispanics enjoy another liberty on those forms which Italian-Americans have not. They get to fill them out in their own language. Most of them arrived in this country after the "speak English and nothing else" tirade has subsided. I am happy that this insanity has ceased. Everyone should be allowed to speak the language of his or her ancestors. (This in the case of many Hispanics would actually be the languages of the Mayans or the Aztecs). Yet, those of us who bothered to learn English may now wish to study the language of the land from which our families immigrated. This may be the single greatest disadvantage to the timing of their arrival. Our language was taken from us. Now, as "culturally enlightened people", we are encouraged to learn yet another foreign tongue so that other groups of newcomers are not forced to learn English.

There is a tie between language and culture that is understood as fundamental by linguists. There are nuances of meaning that resonate through word choices and are unique to certain languages. This is why so many phrases and concepts do not translate directly from one language to another. Language shapes a person's belief system, personality and cognitive process. If you were raised speaking a different language, then you would own an entirely different world view than the one you have now. This is a very difficult concept for monolingual people to understand. However, if you speak a second or even a third language, you are probably nodding your head in agreement as you are reading this.

For the purpose of clarification, let us look at the English language. It is one of the most widely spoken languages in the world. Obviously, this came to pass through aggressive colonization. Yet, why does this persist so long after the fall of the British Empire, growing unpopularity of western culture and staunch grass roots efforts throughout the world to return to native languages?

English is still very much the international business language. It is the language in which deals are made and things get done. I once heard an interesting explanation for this by yet another linguist. English is an "action language"; not every language is. She went on to state that every noun in the English language could be turned into a verb. "Chair?" a woman said. "Chair a meeting", she replied.

"Acne?"

"Chocolate can cause you to acne."

"Globe?"

"Globalize".

The discussion went on.

French, for example, is the international language of diplomacy. I do not speak French myself, but those who do confirm that its very nature is quite diplomatic. Italian, on the other hand, is like hearing music. Its very essence lends itself to creativity and the outpouring of ideas. Look at Italy's history of creativity in the arts and in the sciences. The evidence is all around us. There are a vast number of unchartered accomplishments which were brought into the world by Italian-speaking people. Did the language they were speaking massage the creative nerves of the brain? Did speaking Ancient Greek stroke the philosophical lobes? Linguistic research suggests, "Yes". Is it not possible that being denied the opportunity to learn our native tongue may have stunted our creative as well as our cultural growth?

This question is, of course, rhetorical and the effects are not measurable. Though the answer to this is not tangible, there is another attack on our paisani which is so concrete and malicious it is unimaginable to me that it is still widely denied, but unfortunately, it is. I am referring to the persistent and brazen attacks on Italian-Americans by the mainstream media. They are usually perpetrated in the name of "fun" or "entertainment", as if this makes them less potent. Do not forget that watching Christians being fed to the lions was once a form of entertainment considered fun to watch, by many. People also gathered in village squares for centuries to view hangings, burnings, stonings and firing squad executions. Just because large groups of people find something entertaining does not mean it is harmless.

I doubt there is enough cyber space in the universe on which to list every incident in which Italian-Americans have been defamed by the mainstream media. Even before the "talkie" Italian-Americans were a favorite scapegoat. Silent films such as "The Italian" laid the groundwork for at least one century of the butchering of our character, intellect, culture and style. I grew up watching my beautiful heritage "cartoonized" through the seventies, eighties and nineties. As cultural sensitivity and political correctness emerged, the stereotyping of Italians only intensified. Since, we are "legally White" it seems that we remained a safe punching bag for any racist bully in Hollywood to smack around a little with a script. As members of an "unprotected class" we have no legal recourse when we are targeted for ethnic degradation.

Among the vast archives of such grotesque movies, television, video games, etc., there are some monumental messes that come to mind. Cultural genocide against Italian-Americans is often masked as sensitivity for another culture. Here is an example of a hypocritical dichotomy which is recycled regularly within many a Hollywood script. I remember a cop show from the seventies or eighties which featured a Black cop scolding an Italian man for using the term "broad" in reference to a woman. The writer's underlying message was, "Look how opposed we are to both sexism and racism." Yet, the Italian-American character could not have been depicted in a more foul and stereotypical tone.

As we know, prejudicial portrayals of Italian-Americans have increased and intensified in recent decades partially because writers have had to "lay off" legal minorities. I once heard an analogy in which the deterioration of social media was compared to the art of cooking a frog. It is said that you cannot place a frog in boiling water because the frog will immediately jump out of the pot. But, if you place the frog in "frog temperature" water and gradually turn up the temperature, the frog will allow itself to be cooked. It would now appear that the frog has long passed "al dente". Recently, I have heard Italian men in movies and television being referred to as, "Guidos" and "Gunies" far more frequently. I am sickened by the popularity of shows such as "Jersey Shore", "The Sopranos" and "Mob Wives". I do not know what enrages me more, seeing non-Italians characterize us so repugnantly, (example: Cher's role in "Moonstruck" for which she won an Oscar for a cheap imitation), or seeing John Travolta portraying the idiotic Brooklyn Italian in "Saturday Night Fever" whose speech impediment was never diagnosed or treated. Furthermore, I do not believe I have ever seen a mafia movie in which I did not want to jump through the screen and slap Pacino or De Niro for breathing life into such vile caricatures.

I have challenged non-Italians who either disagree with me or label me as "hypersensitive" to name one reoccurring character of Italian descent in a movie or a television show who is dignified, intelligent and above all articulate. After going through a couple of dozen of disastrous examples, one gentleman blurted out, "Captain Furillo, Hill Street Blues". He then slapped the desk in from of him in some victorious gesture as if he had just "high fived" himself. "That was thirty years ago", I responded. He actually looked embarrassed.

I recently read an interesting article about Samuel Jackson in an Italian-American publication. Jackson refused to play a big role with a large paycheck because he thought the character was demeaning to Black people. Good for him! Where is this integrity on behalf of our Italian-American thespians? I wish some of them would take a lesson from him.

Though the underlying messages in these Italian-American defamation movies are rank and dangerous, most of them do not sport a clear and present social message. They were mainly written and filmed for the sake of entertainment and any social and political messages which they contain are not overt or clearly stated. One exception comes to mind. Unfortunately, there is an American filmmaker who has been awarded over and over for his consistently racist portrayal of Italian-Americans. Most of his films are deemed to have a serious social message. The serious message is usually that Italian-Americans are racist, stupid criminals. I am referring to Spike Lee.

Spike Lee is one of the most highly acclaimed filmmakers of our time. He is lauded by critics for being avant-garde, daring and honest. In truth, almost all of his movies are about racial problems which are perpetrated mostly, if not solely, by Italians. In the movies "Do the Right Thing" and "Summer of Sam" the Italian men all seem to break under pressure toward the end of the story and start yelling senselessly about, "niggers" or "niggers and spics". In truth, this often seems to occur as a non sequitur. "Bronx Tale" is, in my opinion, a film mainly about an ignorant and delinquent Italian-American boy who falls in love with a very nice Black girl and the problems this causes, which are mainly perpetrated by the Italians in the film.

Again, it would not be possible to list every example of Hollywood's bigotry against us. Yet, Spike Lee's work is noteworthy because it exemplifies the level of the "log in your own eye" syndrome which manifests in Hollywood. When he won the Academy Award for, "Do the Right Thing", he was praised repetitively for his "speaking the truth." Of what truth was he speaking? I gather Hollywood's warped version of "the truth" is that Italian-Americans are a bunch of criminal low-lives and that racism continues because of them. This must lift a heavy yoke from the shoulders of every non-Italian in the industry. What a weight off of their shoulders it must be when they place the entire great White burden on ours". Am I speaking of a conspiracy? I am not ruling out the possibility.

Where the big screen, the little screen, print or any other form of media are concerned, another distasteful reality is consistent. Where we are not attacked, we are ignored. In other words, when we are not pulled onto a set to be used as a "whipping post", we are then erased as an entity and simply forgotten. In viewing a commercial, for example, which claims to represent a cross section of women, you will often see one White, one Black, one Hispanic and one Asian woman. The White woman will probably be blonde. If not, you can bet her eyes will be blue. She is readily recognizable as Nordic, Alpine or Anglo-Saxon. Southern Europeans with darker features are almost never chosen to play the role of the Caucasian woman. If you happen to see an Italian-American actor playing the role of a dignified and intelligent "good guy", his character's name will most definitely not end in a vowel. (Names such as "More" and "Neuhause" do not count).

It may be that so many Italian Americans accept being berated because they feel the problem is so ingrained into the behavior patterns of non-Italians that nothing can be done about it. "Why frustrate yourself over something you cannot change?" so to speak. I believe the reason Italian-Americans are not more vocal about being ignored as a distinct population is simply that the only time we are not being ridiculed is when we are not being acknowledged. However, the attempt to erase our distinct identity is a clear and present danger to us on the very genetic level and, as "hokey" as it may sound, we need to fight this by "being who we are".

At this point I would like to divert from the topic and scribe a few words about another group of "White" people that is constantly taunted by Hollywood. Appalachian-Americans, who are primarily of Scottish and Scotch-Irish descent, are flogged by the entertainment industry, almost as regularly as we are. Again, the colossally hypocritical writers would not dream of portraying a "protected class" who could seek legal recompense in such a vile manner. (There are certainly enough lawyers on staff in these giant companies to see to this). Appalachian-Americans, like us, have a rich and fascinating history. Also like us, the most politically correct and "socially enlightened" people, both on and off screen, will stereotype and mimic them mercilessly. (Many of them have never even met a person of this heritage). Yet in their minds, to stereotype a legally recognized minority would be an act of ignorance. In fact, they would probably expect the Appalachian person to do just that.

Once more, we see the brazen cowardice rear its ugly and bigoted head over the Hollywood sign. In all honesty, this case of injustice is much sadder than ours. Appalachia is home to the most unattended pocket of poverty in the country. As Hollywood superstars race all over the world to perform highly publicized acts of philanthropy, the children of the past generations of poor coal miners and small farmers and Revolutionary War soldiers often living in squalor. Not only are they not receiving any help, they are being slandered and characterized for the sake of amusing uninformed audiences who rarely know anything about them. This is beyond insensitive; it's vindictive.

There is a subcategory of disgusting Hollywood releases which surpasses the rest in offensiveness. Again, the list is too long to tackle, but there are a few examples which are too horrifying not to mention. Such low comedy is always destructive, infuriating and perilous, yet the following examples are far worse for one reason. They are written and produced to be viewed by children. I have sighted some noteworthy examples.

I am sure you have heard of the children's cartoon, "Kick Buttowski". It is a name which is hard to forget. Kick Buttowski once played out a "Godfather spoof" in an episode in which Kick went to a restaurant with "Italian" in its name to hire a group of thugs to "take care of" his brother. No one in the establishment could utilize Standard English. Everyone was portrayed as intellectually dim and the only woman on the premises was "big-haired", caked with makeup, smacking gum and filing her nails.

I have seen similar portrayals in many a Disney Channel show including "Sonny with a Chance" and "Hannah Montana", in more than one episode. Any college freshman who has taken psych 101 can tell you that any behavior which is repeated is motivated. In conclusion, these attacks are not without a malicious agenda. There are also more subtle but more frequently placed ethnic slams sprinkled throughout the episodes of many other Disney Channel shows.

One such example which aired on an episode of "The Sweet Life on Deck" comes to mind. A group of teenagers is sitting around discussing the mysterious new student in their class. One of them suggests, "Maybe he's in the witness protection program." (The boy is obviously of African descent). Another student replies, "He doesn't exactly look like a 'goodfella' ". Canned laughter is then released and the stereotype of the Italian-American mobster is reinforced in our youth. In translation, mobsters never look African, Irish, Jewish, Chinese, Russian, etc., only Italian.

I have not seen everything that Disney has to offer mainly because my daughter's television time has always been limited. I am, however, experienced enough to know that, "Where there's smoke, there's fire." The examples of Disney Channel's negative depiction of Italian-Americans that I have listed are probably only the "tip of the iceberg". Furthermore, I have also never encountered a positive and dignified Italian-American or Italian character on this network, or on any other network for that matter. This is particularly offensive given that Disney considers itself to be progressive, multi-cultural and politically correct. They are constantly celebrating a wide array of culturally diverse children and very respectfully teaching the rest of us about their cultures. We, however, are only recognized to be poked fun at. We are not even absorbed into the pool of waspy characters on the shows. We are simply written out of the stories and then pulled in as a ridiculous sideshow upon command.

Another child entertainment giant which conducts its self like a gigantic hypocrite is American Girl. They claim to be portraying a cross section of American girls with diverse backgrounds, but once again we are passed over. American Girl Dolls are Black, Anglo-Saxon White, Jewish, Hispanic, Asian, Native-American and several other ethnicities. Once again, the fifth largest ethnic group in America is not represented.

I feel strongly that the previous examples of bigotry are worth sighting because these child entertainment giants are poisoning our youth. The most tender of Italian-Americans are seeing their precious legacy dragged through the mud for the amusement of the ignorant. Also, non-Italian children are being served the same stale hemlock which has been poured up by the entertainment industry for more than a century. It may be stale, but it is still toxic. It must stop and it is up to us to make it stop!

I am imploring every Italian-American to select one company, one network or one publication and make some noise. Stir it up! Many

Italian-Americans complain that non-Italians will not listen. I think the larger problem is that Italians will not talk. I have had conversations about this with non-Italians who have dismissed me callously. I have also spoken to a fewer number of them who listened to me open-mindedly and came to some realizations. We are not going to repair a lifetime of socially and media induced damage done to a mind in one conversation. We of all people should understand that "Rome wasn't built in a day". Yet, prejudice is learned behavior which means it can be unlearned, so start teaching.

While selecting a media based company to "go for the jugular" on, I would like to suggest to anyone with young children or grandchildren that Disney Channel and American Girl are excellent choices. If for no other reason, you need to inventory and repair the damage all of this exclusion and ridicule has done to their little psyches. Also, there is a wonderful lesson here in how to stand up to a bully. Remember, (going back to basic psychology again), if a message is repeated enough we have a tendency to believe it. We cannot have our future believing that we are not unique in any way other than that we are absurd.

In addition to portraying Italians and Italian-Americans as dishonest, hot tempered and of dull intellect, there is another prevalent stereotype which disturbs me more than the others. I have no doubt that it is the influence of the media which causes the unenlightened masses to view Italians and Italian-Americans as comical by nature. Strange bursts of inappropriate laughter often spring forth from non-Italians in response to hearing anything Xenocentric to Italians. This is a highly peculiar phenomenon. In addition to perpetrating vicious stereotypes about us, the host culture has managed to distort the most beautiful aspects of our heritage and has programed the unenlightened masses to metabolize anything Italian as a "Three Stooges" episode.

I have personally told non-Italians about my culture, traditions and heritage and been received with bizarre and inappropriately placed laughter. I have even told people I am Italian and had them chuckle. Why?

There is an old Italian church in Chicago which is committed to teaching our traditions to its youngest parishioners. The church holds a beautiful mass on the epiphany in which the priest calls the children up to the beautifully decorated altar, sits them down and tells them the story of the Befana. During the mass, the soloist sings the most enchanting Italian Christmas songs and the children are invited to sing along. Afterwards, the Befana herself enters the church and tells the children her story. She then passes out gifts to all of them and she walks out with the procession.

We took our daughter to this mass every year since she was three until she was ten. This day is something we look forward to each year. The night before the Epiphany, we read the story of "La Befana" and she puts her shoes out to be filled with "goodies". Now, she reads it to us and has no intention of giving up the practice no matter how old she is.

I once explained this tradition to an Anglo-Saxon neighbor. I was beaming with warmth and pride as I described each facet of the celebration to her. Sadly, the woman could not appreciate my story because she was too busy laughing at it. She laughed a guttural and pitchy laugh. Its tone was that of someone hearing something they thought was ridiculous, yet made them slightly uncomfortable, at the same time.

The entire time I was enduring this brazen act of disrespect, I had the feeling that if I had told her that this was the practice of any other ethnicity, she would have listened respectfully and given positive feedback. You see, like so many who "bash" us, this woman deems herself to be very politically correct and enlightened. I have also informed several others of a similar mindset that my daughter takes Italian lessons and attends an Italian language summer camp. I have experienced the same weird laughter in response to this and also the "stony" poker face of disapproval. Sometimes the laughter is a chuckle and other times it is more of an idiotic outburst. All of these reactions lead me to believe that something about the retrieval of our culture makes some people very uncomfortable.

What is the source of this deep-seeded discomfort? As we know we can, in part, thank our friends in Hollywood again for persistently berating us at every turn. Yet, there are other ingredients in this racist recipe. We were the first very large voluntary wave of non-Anglo-Saxon immigrants into this country. This was undoubtedly seen as a threat to the host culture and spiked the militant movement to force ethnic Whites to assimilate completely into what they considered to be American culture. There was extreme pressure to abandon everything from which we emerged. Unfortunately many of our second generation forefathers played into this; it was not a possibility for our first generation ancestors. I will address this in greater detail, later on. In spite of all attempts by the host culture to "whitewash" our distinctiveness, we were changing the flavor of the American landscape in many ways. This spawned fear and even hostility.

WHEN ITALIAN-AMERICANS BEGAN ARRIVING IN AMERICA IN LARGE NUMBERS, DISCRIMINATION WAS LEGAL AND THRIVING.

When I was a child, my cousins' nonna, a Sicilian immigrant raised in Texas, told me a chilling story of how her entire family was forced to move out her childhood home in the middle of the night when the landlord found out that they were Italian. She may or may not have realized this but at that place and time, Italians were the second most likely ethnic group to be victims of lynching. We all know who was unfortunate enough to be in first place. We know because it has been heavily publicized that the Ku Klux Clan was lynching Black victims on a regular basis. The largest public lynching in American history was perpetrated against a group of Italian men in New Orleans in 1891. By some accounts there were nineteen victims and by some there were twenty-one. Yet, very few Americans, both Italian and non-Italian have ever heard of the incident.

Though the movie industry did not yet exist, we were already victims of media generated prejudice. New Orleans newspapers regularly ran political cartoons depicting the "dago" as lazy, dim-witted and delinquent. If you have any doubt that these publications helped pave the way to the lynchings, read up a little on genocide. Scholars in the area of genocide diligently study the social conditions in locations in which genocide has occurred in the years directly preceding the incidents. Propaganda and plenty of it is a crucial precursor to such atrocities. In Rwanda for example, inflammatory songs about the Tutsi people were being played by radio stations for several years before the massive genocide occurred. Hitler also used radio to brainwash his population into believing that the Jews were the key to all of Germany's problems in the years which followed the Treaty of Versailles. In both of these cases of actual genocide, the conditioning took place over a period of time. The negative messages about the victims' races were repeated over and over, thus the term "conditioning". I would argue that Italian-Americans have fallen victim to a "cultural genocide", largely induced by the media. The relentless attacks on every aspect of our being has caused the widespread death of our cultural identity as well as the emergence of a grotesque stereotype which far too many of our people accept and even live out due to this brainwashing.

One of the strangest results of this constant distortion of our culture by the entertainment industry I mentioned earlier. I am referring to the preposterous misperception that the Italian mafia is the only mafia. Of course, Italians have a mafia. Given that we were at one time the largest and most dramatically oppressed European-American ethnic group in the country, it became very large. Yet, every ethnicity had a mafia and they still do. Now, however, we have to be careful not to offend anyone,

anyone other than us, that is. At the time of the Italian mafia's heyday, there were two other Caucasian mafias which were just as big, just as mean and just as powerful. They were never, however, just as publicized or just as incarcerated. These were the Jewish and the Irish mafias.

I made a reference to a neighbor the other day about the "Irish Mob". This woman, who calls herself educated responded, "I thought they were Italian". After this, I made it a point to strike up a conversation with anyone I could and mention the "Irish mafia". I was flabbergasted to see how many people did not know what I was talking about. The strangest thing of all is that I live in Chicago. How could anyone live in this city, above all others, and be completely unaware of the existence of this crime ring?

Again, I live in Chicago. Therefore, the Irish mob is of particular interest to me. The Irish implanted themselves in the political institutions in this country early on. They were able to saturate the executive, legislative and judicial branches of local government early on. The Jewish mafia infiltrated the entertainment industry in its infancy. Of course, the news publications of this era continued their tradition of quickly printing anything that perpetrated the idea that Italians were the sole criminals of the era. Even the Anglocentric history books have taken part in the rhetorical bloodshed.

THE DEFAMATION OF THE ITALIAN-AMERICAN IS THOROUGH AND BEGINS BY ASSAULTING ITALIAN CULTURE IN ITS PRENATAL STAGE.

I am referring to the Roman Empire. In spite of all of the accomplishments of this regime, it is predominantly remembered for its acts of brutality and barbarism. The Romans, for example, had indoor plumbing. Modern engineers marvel at the aqueducts and at the fact that many of Roman roads are still in use. The Romans ushered in urban life, the Latin school model and more than dabbled in an early form of globalism. The writings of Cicero and the navigational breakthroughs of the Mediterranean are unknown to many people. They do, however, know that those nasty Romans crucified Jesus and fed a bunch of people to the lions.

All of this did, of course, occur. These were brutal times and human rights arguments were not yet on the table. If you conquered a group of people, you made them into slaves and the Romans were winning at the time. This means they conquered a lot of people. This was a dreadful reality. The Ancient Romans certainly were a violent culture. Yet, behind every great empire there was a violent way of life. Anyone who has studied the Greeks, Carthaginians, or Egyptians will tell you that they were no less violent and their punishments and tactics were not any gentler. Why is it that they are not yoked with the same barbaric reputation?

If you were to travel a little over a hundred miles north on the Italian peninsula, you will find the remains from a lesser known civilization. The Etruscans were iron workers. They are credited with the inventions of the fork and false teeth. The Etruscans were known for high fashion, ingenuity and enterprise. They were also known for treating their slaves very well. This may sound peculiar to your twenty-first century consciousness, but in the ancient world, this was a huge act of humanitarianism. Still, their offspring would, arguably consist of a disproportionate number of geniuses, including Dante, da Vinci, Michelangelo, Galileo and Marconi. Now, the kindness and gentleness of one group whose descendants would become the Italians is not recognized. Only the brutality of another group of people whose descendants would become the Italians is noted. The genius of either of these ancient peoples is rarely emphasized.

I want to "fast forward" about one and one half millennia to discuss an Italian who, once again is being remembered for his violence rather than his brilliance. His accomplishments are being written out of the history books and replaced with tales of his brutality. I am referring to

Christopher Columbus. Christopher Columbus is on his way to being recognized only as the lunatic who jumped off his boat in the Bahamas swinging a machete and demanding gold from the natives. I will not attempt to excuse or to justify everything done by Columbus in the Americas, nor do I approve of it. The fact remains that he was a key player in linking America to the "Old World", he proved a scientific concept which would change history and denying his accomplishments is another form of the "cultural genocide" of which I am writing.

The first thing we need to remember while entertaining any thoughts about Columbus is that he sailed for the Spanish Crown. In order to fully understand the influence this had on his actions and the unfairness of the attempt to disintegrate his accomplishments, let us first review the conquests of a couple of other explorers who sailed under the same sponsorship.

Hernando Cortez was the chief magistrate of Santiago, Hispaniola, (There is that word again!). He was married into the Spanish royal family and was known for brutally working the natives in the mines. It was once written of him, "How many Indians died in extracting gold for him? God will have kept a better account than I."

Upon the discovery of Mexico by Spanish explorers, Cortez was sent by the Spanish crown with an expedition for the purpose of conquering the land and the kingdom. His group sailed from Cuba and landed on the shores of Tabasco. When he encountered his first natives he demanded of them, "Does your king have any gold?" It is said that he went on to explain that he had a disease of the heart which could only be cured by the acquisition of gold.

This infection was no doubt the plague of the Spanish throne itself. The quest for precious metals was a driving force in the launching of the Spanish expeditions. Cortez then ordered the natives to bring him their king as well as their gold. As history tells us, the Aztec people were then enslaved, tortured, raped, and murdered both before and after the fall of the Montezuma Kingdom. Where is the movement to rename the Sea of Cortez and remove his name from the history books? It seems that every act of violence committed by Cortez in Mexico was basically mirrored by Pizarro in Peru in abuses against the Incan civilization. Again, I am not aware of any attempt underway to undermine his legacy.

Although the Spanish colonized the largest portion of the Americas, we are certainly aware that the English, French, Dutch and Portuguese were here, as well. Many are not aware, however, that the Italians were present on this side of the globe, also. I am not referring to Christopher Columbus. The explorer John Cabot, who discovered North America, in 1497, while sailing under the English flag was actually, Giovanni Caboto, another Italian explorer. Actually, the first known Italian settlers in the colonies were the "Tagliaferro" family. This family of glassblowers set up shop in Jamestown, Virginia in 1637. Their name was soon changed to "Tolliver" and is still well-known throughout the south. The American Southwest and California were mapped, almost entirely by an Italian named "Eusebio Kino" and the route to the source of the Mississippi was discovered by another "paisano" by the name of "Giacomo Costantino Beltrami". Undoubtedly, we were not only present, but very proactive in the colonization of this continent. Never forget, that the mass of land on which we reside was named for the Italian mapmaker, Amerigo Vespucci.

In colonial times, there was a very small group of Italians living right here in the middle of North America in the thirteen colonies. There were very small in numbers, were primarily of Tuscan origin and made some significant contributions to the formation of this country.

In 1773, Filippo Mazzei, an Italian physician, led a group of Italians from his native Tuscany to Virginia. Their purpose was to cultivate olives, vineyards and various fruits on this continent. Mazzei was successful in doing this on a small scale. Most importantly, he accomplished this in the absence of slave labor. Instead, he employed Tuscan farmers, who sailed over with their vines in hand.

Actually, Dr. Mazzei was very strongly opposed to slavery. Given his intellectual nature and his proximity to "Monticello," (the estate of Thomas Jefferson), the two naturally became good friends. In fact, Jefferson who was enamored of Italian culture often translated documents into English for Mazzei. One such document included the phrase, "All men are by nature free and equal". The phrase was written and signed by Mazzei several years before Jefferson wrote the Declaration of Independence, which as you know includes the phrase, "All men are created equal". Do you happen to see a blunt force undeniable resemblance between the two phrases? Thomas Jefferson came from a wealthy slave-owning Virginia family. He grappled with the morality of his station in life and did release his slaves on his deathbed. Was it because of Dr. Mazzei that he had a change of heart? This is certainly feasible.

Jefferson had vowed to release his slaves upon the adoption of the Constitution. Unfortunately, the "all men are created equal" clause was not enough to bring on emancipation. Other verbiage which would have forced the end of slavery was stricken from the document. This was a condition imposed by the southern states. They refused to sign before the deletion of such language and without a unanimous vote. Hence, independence would not be an option. Thus, the issue of abolition was forced onto the back burner.

The phrase "all men are created equal", however, did not go unrewarded. It was sighted in arguments for both the "Emancipation Proclamation" and the "Civil Rights Amendment". I would say that Thomas Jefferson should only be given partial credit for this. Filippo Mazzei should be honored, as well. I am sure that Hollywood will not be filming the life story of "Filippo Mazzei: Doctor, Writer, Agriculturist, Early American and Civil Rights Champion", any time soon.

In addition to Dr. Mazzei, I would like to mention two of his contemporaries who were also of Italian heritage. Each of these men has actually earned the title, "Founding Father". The first is William Paca. He was a representative to the Continental Congress and one of the founders of "The Sons of Liberty". He is also remembered as a staunchly opposed to slavery. His signature is on the Declaration of Independence.

There is another gentleman of Italian heritage whose signature is on the Declaration of Independence. His name is Caesar Rodney. Rodney was, very much, the unsung hero of the Continental Congress. Without Caesar Rodney, there may have never been a United States of America.

Caesar Rodney was descended from the prominent Tuscan family, the Adelmares of Treviso. By most accounts, he was the fourth generation out of Italy and his family had settled in England before coming to the colony of Delaware. Rodney was an avid activist for the cause of independence. Delaware had two other representatives and they were divided on the issue. One was pro-independence and the other was a loyalist.

As I mentioned earlier, independence from England was to be declared only by a unanimous vote. This meant that each state had to vote for independence and not that each representative had to do so. There was one more stipulation and that was that every man had to be present to vote. No proxy votes could be cast. A split vote would sway to the side of caution which would mean that state's vote would be counted against independence. Caution certainly does not mean revolution.

To further complicate the matter, Cesar Rodney was escorted home several days prior to the final vote. He was sick with cancer and was brought home to die in his own bed. The news reached Rodney that unanimity of states was to be required for declaring independence. He arose from what was assumed to be his deathbed and rode eighty miles in a thunderstorm sick with asthma and cancer in order to sign the declaration. I am seeing that we were not only present at the birth of our nation; we were at the very least among the midwives.

As in the case of Christopher Columbus, there is an attempt to undermine the accomplishments of another Italian contributor to the formation of America. His name is Paul Revere. Yes, Paul Revere was Italian. Paul Revere's father was Apollus Riviore. He anglicized his name to "Revere" to better fit in in Boston. There are several erroneous sources which say that Paul Revere was French. This is not correct. He was a cousin on Caesar Rodney and was most certainly of Italian heritage. He was, as is frequently pointed out, not the only rider on that infamous night in Boston. He was, however, the master mind behind the system in play on that evening.

Revere worked as a bell ringer in the North Church. He was active in publicizing and protesting the Boston Massacre and made innumerable contributions to the patriotic movement. His painting of the Boston Massacre is criticized for leaving out the attack on Crispus Attucks. He did this because he was trying to gain sympathy from the British crown in an attempt to bring the guilty redcoats to justice. He also dressed the other victims in the picture as noblemen and not the apprentices that they were. He did this also to increase the chances of obtaining justice. As for the criticism that he was not the only one who made the "midnight ride", he never claimed that he was. It was Henry Wadsworth Longfellow who implied as much in his famous poem, "The Midnight Ride".

Although the numbers of Italians in the thirteen colonies were low, these early Italian settlers were, generally, highly educated, of higher socioeconomic class and very well respected. Our numbers had increased slightly by the time of the Civil War. During the war, there were four Italian generals and Italians were the fourth most represented foreign ethnicity on the battlefield. In fact, President Lincoln offered command of a key regiment to General Garibaldi in the beginning of the war due to his stellar achievements in fighting Brazil's War of Independence. Garibaldi declined. He did so because, at the beginning of the war, President Lincoln had not yet issued an official statement stating that the main purpose of the war was to free the slaves. By the time the Emancipation Proclamation was adopted, Garibaldi was fast at work in Italy fighting for its unification. Like Mazzei, Garibaldi was fiercely opposed to slavery. This is yet another irony, given our Hollywood inflicted stereotypes.

In the year following the Civil War, Italian immigrants surged into the United States. We tend to think of the early Italian immigrant as surrounded by the bustle of New York, Boston, Chicago and other big cities in the North. The majority of our nonni and bisnonni certainly fell into this setting, but there were some who settled in the south. They did so just in time to feel the pangs of the White supremacist movement, which of course was fueled by the repercussions of the Civil War. As I stated earlier they were often lynched, killed in coal mine explosions, performed grueling labor as farmhands and suffered many other abuses. Italians being "Papists" further ignited the hatred in the clansmen who had been saturated with Calvinist propaganda for generations.

Though greater in numbers, life was certainly not a "bowl of cherries" for the Italian immigrant in the northern states either. In addition to being far removed from the host culture by language, appearance and religion, he probably disembarked at Ellis Island with another burden in tote. The "patrone" or patron system further salted the wounds of poverty on the backs of many an Italian immigrant, at the time. Much like the indentured servants, we all learned of when we studied our nation's colonial period in school, our Italian forefathers frequently bore a similar ball and chain.

In the late eighteen hundreds, Italy was also enduring a post-civil war economy. Their economic "slump" was actually far worse than that of our post-war south. Former American slave, Booker T. Washington, visited Southern Italy during this period. He later wrote, "The Negro is not the man furthest down." He was referring to the southern Italian. In addition to ever growing unemployment in the small country, inflation was out of control. The result was mass exodus from southern Italy. Furthermore, the "type" of Italian who immigrated into this country had changed drastically. The descendants of the colonists who welcomed the well-off Tuscan landowner were not nearly as hospitable to the poor Sicilian laborer; nor were other European immigrants and ethnic groups.

Thus, the average Italian immigrant was completely destitute and could not pay his passage to the New World. (Seventy-eight percent of them were men). Hence, the patron/patrone would pick up the cost of the voyage. He would also find employment for the newcomer. In exchange for the service, the patron took the entire wage of the laborer and doled him out a very small allowance. As you can imagine, the exploitation was of monumental proportion.

Nonetheless, Little Italys materialized sharply and swelled quickly. Bigoted press towards Italians, as we know, was frequent and flagrant. Though the majority of these publications were equally grotesque, I located one release, in particular that disturbs me more than the others. It does so not because of what was said, but by whom it was said. The article was published in "Catholic World". The writer argued that Italians had a style of worship which was so different to that of the Irish that they were not actually Catholic. It went on to cast disapproval upon the use of saints favored by Italians for intercessory prayer and implied that all of their practices were resulting from ignorance, lack of intelligence and a more primitive nature than their paler counterparts.

The article, which again appeared in "Catholic World" in 1888 and was written by Bernard Lynch, who went on to say that his neighborhood and his parish had been invaded by "dark haired, olive tinted men and women".

There were a few exceptional Irish lay people and clergy who assisted the needy newcomers and they deserve to be recognized. Father Daniel Burke and heiress Annie Geary fought hard against the prejudice. Sadly, they were exceptions and not the norm. Overall, the existing Irish and German founded Catholic churches in this country were unwelcoming to and often intolerant of the Italian Catholic.

In fact, many predominantly Irish and German parishes cast their Italian parishioners into the basement to worship. Being sent to the church basement must feel a lot like being sent to the back of the bus. (I have recently seen a lot of publicity implying that the Irish single-handedly built the Catholic Church in this country). Philosophically, however, the Catholic Church is to be the universal church, not the church in which people who look different and worship in a different language are sent away. So, in addition to being charged through Ellis Island (or the island of tears, as some called it) like cattle, names changed and identities plundered, worked senselessly with sub-poverty level compensation, preyed upon by criminals and treated like some sort of sub-human life form, the church, which should have been a beacon of light was mistreating us. Can you imagine what a horrific shock it must have been for these devout Italian Catholics, who had had the church as refuge since their infancy, to suddenly be thrown out of it?

Our proud forefathers responded with character and ingenuity. Since they were not welcome in the "Catholic" churches built by the Irish and Germans, they constructed many a stunning cathedral-like "Romocentric" Catholic church throughout the country. Our nonni and bisnonni toiled for long hours in the sweat shops of the time. They then returned to their neighborhoods and constructed these monumental houses of worship at night. The men often worked until they dropped. Some of these men were employed building our nation's skyscrapers by day. They picked up their welding torches. Others employed their ice carts. Women carried bricks in their aprons and children worked alongside them. They were willing to work at any price necessary in order to have a spiritual home, once again.

Although the bigotry and poverty in this country could at times be crippling, Italians here managed to form tightly knit communities and preserve quite a bit of their culture on the new continent. The little Italys in American cities were complete with cafes, Italian newspapers, markets complete with all of the culinary necessities and opera stages. Yet, make no mistake; times were very hard. Food was often scarce and Italians worked the most dangerous and low-paying jobs. Additionally, they were often the victims of brutal crimes at the hands of those outside their communities.

One of Chicago's Little Italys was referred to as "Little Hell" by outsiders due to its overcrowding and poor living conditions. Italian Harlem or East Harlem was another example of the ghastly living conditions our forefathers endured. At the time these tenements were constructed, there were no laws pertaining to leaving any outdoor space on a property. Hence, if you were an Italian-American child in the neighborhood, you played on the street if you could find the room. Neither a yard nor a park were available to you. In fact, conditions remained so poor for so long that as late as the 1960's, sixty percent of the residents in these communities were without private toilets and eighty-four percent were without central heat.

If Catholic schools could talk, they would tell a similar story. Italian children were not always welcome in the Irish founded Catholic schools. This is truly a tragic irony. Elizabeth Seton founded the first Catholic school in America because Catholic children were not welcome in public schools, at the time. It seems that the Italian children were unwelcome to receive an education with the other "unwelcome" children of the time. Consequently, in addition to churches, we had to build parish schools.

Discrimination at the university level was even worse. Italian and Italian-American scholars and educators stepped up to the plate and began to establish Catholic universities across the country. This was yet another long hard journey, but the harvest was bountiful. The result was a vast network of Catholic colleges and universities throughout the nation which are still thriving today. A disproportionate number of our Catholic institutions of higher learning in this country were founded by Italian and Italian-American scholars.

At the beginning of the twentieth century, our numbers rose on this continent as more and more people left the motherland in seek of relief from the harsh circumstances in southern Europe. As our numbers increased, the onset of an even more chilling type of bigotry was on deck. Our involvement in World War I cultivated a climate ripe for a movement for American isolationism. This was the beginning of the long lived "speak only English and be only American" movement, from which many of us are still feeling the aftershocks. After the war, the discrimination would intensify, due to the surge of organized crime due to prohibition. Though the Italian mafia was present and powerful during the era, the political systems as well as the news and entertainment industries would focus so heavily on the Italian mafia, that many people of that and future generations would not even realize that other powerful mafias did and still do exist. (Remember my neighbor I mentioned at the beginning of the book who thought ALL mobsters are Italian).

To fathom the formation of the Italian mafia, one must first understand a small bit about the history of Sicily. In short, it is an island which is placed in a very vulnerable location. This was most unfortunate in the ancient world. Every ancient empire with access to the Mediterranean trampled Sicily -- the Greeks, the Romans, the Carthaginians, the Egyptians, etc. Sicilians were caught up in a cycle that lasted for millennia of being ruled by outsiders that could neither have been more disinterested in their welfare, nor the future of the island. Consequently, they banded together and formed secret societies which were initially put into play to resist and survive the invading forces. If an individual did not respect or abide by the laws laid down by the current regime, it did not reflect poorly upon a member's honor. Given the invaders' treatment of the Sicilians, their laws were not expected to be followed.

According to the FBI, (a dubious source, at best), it was not until the 1920's that the mafia turned "wicked". The social conditions in this country for the Italian certainly set the stage for their mafia's involvement in the "roaring twenties". One would think, by reading their files that no one else was involved in "bootlegging". I once heard a comedian say that FBI actually stands for "Forever Bothering Italians". Once again, these less upstanding Italian-American citizens are grossly overrepresented in popular culture. The other key players in the crime scene of the 1920's were the Irish and Jewish mafias.

Most sources are in agreement that the Irish mafia's presence in this country predates that of the Italian mafia by almost half a century. There are a couple of films which come to mind that showcase John Dillinger and Bugs Moran. Yet again, their memory is dwarfed by the long scroll of Italian mafia movies which Hollywood continues to churn out on this racially motivated assembly line. The truth of the matter is that America has a very "diverse" mafia heritage.

In addition to the Irish mafia having been in America first, they were also entirely composed of native English speakers. They set their sights primarily on gaining a stronghold on the nation's political systems, in order to operate their crime rings freely. All of our older and major cities were, and in many cases are still, controlled by Irish mafia politicians. New York, Boston and Chicago are perfect examples. From the beat cop to the mayor, these cities were controlled and operated by the Irish mafia. The Irish mobsters and those working within their systems understood the growing threat of the increasing Italian population as well as the rise of the Italian "operation". The animosity increased.

Old Italian-American gentlemen who have grown up within the city limits of Chicago have told me that when they were children, Irish cops would stop and ask them if they were Italian. If they responded, "Yes", they would receive a hard slap across the face. This would be followed with a slur such as, "No good Guinea!" or "Stupid Wop!"

As vile as abuses of this caliber may seem, particularly against children, the perils of being Italian in United States were far greater than the possibility of enduring a humiliating "crack in the puss", here and there. For instance, in continuing the topic of the Irish mafia, it was very easy for this crime ring to commit illegal acts and then "pin them" on whatever Italian or Italians were convenient, at the time. Remember, the police departments were largely controlled by the Irish mob. They decided what reports were written, who was indicted for what and what information was released to the press. Hence, the Irish thugs could "pull off a job" and the Irish police departments would name a suspect from the "Italian outfit", or even a law abiding Italian, in many cases. The rest would run its course, but certainly not without intervention. This being said, I am not alone in believing that the Saint Valentine's Day Massacre is an epic example of this strategy in play.

Before this infamous event, Al Capone's public image was quite different. The onset of the Great Depression brought immeasurable despair to the entire nation. The pangs of hunger were particularly painful throughout the nation's Italian neighborhoods. One might say that the stock market crashed directly into Italian East Harlem in 1929. More than half of the neighborhood was without work, starvation was rampant and citizens of Italian heritage were less likely to receive aid of any kind than were members of the mainstream culture.

Al Capone stepped up to the plate and became known for quite a few large-scale acts of charity. He set up numerous soup kitchens at the beginning of the great depression and founded and financed an organization which distributed milk to school children in an attempt to fight rickets. It is said that he aided many a destitute Italian when no one else would help them and asked for nothing in return. However, Capone was "getting huge", he was posing a serious threat to the Irish mob and they were desperate to stop him.

On February 14, 1929, seven men associated with Bugs Moran's north side gang were gunned down in cold blood in a garage located at 2122 N. Clark Street in Chicago. The crime has become an iconic event in the archives of the Chicago mob. While examining this crime, keep in mind that mobsters kill regularly within their own gangs. It is commonplace for members of all of the mafias to "brush off" those who might be in line for the same promotion or those who they believe have been disloyal to them.

According to the newspapers of the time, the seven men who were gunned down were members of Moran's gang. Moran himself was conveniently late for a meeting in the garage with a prominent bootlegger in which he would have exchanged cash for hundreds of cases or whiskey to sell in his speakeasies. Now, the gunmen were reportedly from Capone's gang. (Al Capone himself was in Miami for the winter at the time of the assassinations). They were said to have stolen police uniforms and even a police car to complete the job. So, these suspiciously Italian-looking policemen supposedly sauntered into the Moran-operated garage, lined up seven of his thugs and filled them full of bullets without any resistance whatsoever. Afterwards, they walked out two of their associates in the act who were no longer wearing the uniform. They held guns to their backs to give the appearance that they were being arrested. Supposedly, these Sicilian mobsters were taken for Irish cops by everyone who saw them walking in and out of the garage and not one witness raised an eyebrow at their "non-coplike" features.

Remember, this was not one of the ethnically diverse communities in which we reside today.

Another compelling detail in the archives of the Saint Valentine's Day Massacre is that no one was ever indicted for the crime. The annals of Chicago history would have us believe that these accounts of impersonating police officers and stealing a police car went unindicted, not to mention the seven murder charges. In contemplating the logistics of the "hit", it is clear to me that the Irish mob already had access to the police car and uniforms. Some of them would not have even had to change their clothes before performing the job. Although Chicago's finest said they did not have enough evidence to indict a guilty party, they released Capone's name to the press as the perpetrator.

The national attention that this crime brought to Capone and his gang put him in a position where the "feds" were watching his every move. Eventually, he landed in Alcatraz on charges of tax evasion. It was Capone's absence due to incarceration that empowered the Irish North Side Gang and enabled them to really "rope in" the entire Chicago black market and fine tune the city's political machine.

Though many may find it challenging to "conjure up" any compassion for career criminals who have been falsely accused (particularly when no jail time was served), the majority of the victims of this system were not law-breakers. They were good Italian people who, again, were in the wrong place at the wrong time. One such tragic incident was the case of Bartolomeo Vanzetti and Nicola Sacco. These two men were falsely convicted for the murders of Frederick Parmenter and Alessandro Berardelli. The two victims were bringing boxes filled with payroll into a shoe factory, when they were robbed and killed. The murder was blamed on Vanzetti and Sacco, who were both Italian immigrants. They were also both politically outspoken and very involved in the Socialist Party. Perhaps, some viewed this as a threat and welcomed their removal from society.

Both men had ironclad alibis as to where they were at the time of the crime. Vanzetti was in Plymouth selling fish and Sacco was in Boston having a family portrait taken. This was a lengthy process, at the time. These solid alibis were dismissed by the judge in the case because, "all of the witnesses were Italian". Sacco and Vanzetti were both convicted and sentenced to death.

Two years prior to their execution, a Portuguese mafia member confessed that his gang had orchestrated the crime and described the process in detail. Nevertheless, the execution took place as scheduled. Furthermore, only two of the witnesses produced by the prosecution were able to identify Sacco and Vanzetti and then only in as much as they "looked Italian". Apparently, that was enough for this "Waspy" judge to take their lives.

The case gained national attention and was written about by some of the most prominent "muckrakers" of the era. This list included Upton Sinclair, George Bernard Shaw, H.G. Wells and Jane Adams. All of those listed became actively involved in an effort to obtain a retrial of the case. Judge Webster Thayer was criticized by many for his conduct throughout the trial. Still, the authorities would not rescind his decision to execute the men.

On August 23rd, 1927, these two innocent men were executed. Over 250,000 people protested this injustice in Boston as protests rang out simultaneously in European countries. In Paris, a bomb which killed twenty people went off in protest of the executions.

Though the case of Sacco and Vanzetti is a gut wrenching example of the abuses our judicial system has heaped upon us, it is far from a rarity. Though this particular case gained notoriety through the quill and industry of some socially responsible writers of the era, far too many similar cases went unnoticed. Just how many Italians served as a "patsy" to a crime, is something we will probably never know. If we did, I am sure that the numbers would be daunting.

Finally, fifty years after the murders of Vanzetti and Sacco, Governor Michael Dukakis of Massachusetts ordered a full investigation into the horrific event. The two men were deemed innocent and an apology was issued by the state. Unfortunately, there was very little media attention given to the event and not much public interest was generated.

At the onset of WWII, prejudice against Italian-Americans intensified. In many places the isolationism movement was taken a step further and it became illegal to speak Italian. On the national scale, the federal government printed posters which read, "Don't speak the enemy's language". They went on to explain that Italian, German and Japanese should never be spoken in public because crucial information may be leaked out to a spy who could be lurking nearby, at any time. I have to laugh at this. Crucial information about what -- my grandmother's grocery list? As comical as this may seem, at the time there was a very high level of paranoia amongst the public. Everyone seems to be aware of the grave injustice suffered by Japanese-Americans of the era. Few realize that Italian-Americans suffered an identical fleecing of their civil liberties.

The Japanese inhabitants of the WWII internment camps received a formal apology from the federal government as well as a monetary compensation, in many cases. There is a monument on Ellis Island in their honor with a sentiment posted to the suggestion that we must not ever forget what happened to these American citizens. I would like to go on record as saying; I agree. This is a social injustice that should be acknowledged. Yet, our forefathers of this generation suffered a similar plight; and no one seems to know anything about it.

Preceding the onset of our involvement in the war in Europe and Africa, more than ten thousand Italian-Americans, then living in California, were also forcefully and quickly removed from their homes. About thirty-two hundred of them landed in internment camps in Fort Lincoln, North Dakota, Chrystal City, Texas, Missoula, Montana and

McAlister, Oklahoma. Tens of thousands more were simply cast out of their cities and communities and forced into homelessness. Given that they were often immigrants, many of them had no place to go. I read a story about one woman who became so desperate she forced to take shelter in a chicken coop.

Quite a few of the Italians who were "forced out" in California were fishermen. After the bombing of Pearl Harbor, Franklin Roosevelt reinstated the Espionage Act of 1917. This act allows federal, state and local government to "throw due process rights to the wind" and confiscate any foreign vessel that enters our waters for suspicion of sedition and conspiracy. This is where the situation became convoluted. Many of the "small time" fishermen in California were Italian immigrants who were awaiting naturalization. Through the distortion of this act, the government not only "sent them packing", but they first confiscated their boats. There were two thousand of these unlucky fishermen in the city of Pittsburg, California. Many fishermen throughout other parts of California, including San Francisco, suffered the same injustice. One of these victims happened to be the father of baseball legend Joe DiMaggio.

The west coast Italians who were permitted to retain their residences did not sail through this bigotry without hardship. California placed rigid restrictions upon their comings and goings. No Italian was allowed to travel out of a five mile radius from his or her home and all night travel was forbidden. As you can imagine, these rules cost them many a job. Yet, the stipulations did not stop there. The immigrants also had their flashlights and radios taken away and were forced to carry a card which identified them as Italian. Now, this seems to mirror some of Hitler's escapades on the "other side of the pond" verbatim. We were, at the time, already somewhat aware of his reign of terror because so many prudent European Jews heeded the warning this brought and came to the States for refuge. Yet, we copied the injustice and perpetrated it against one of our minorities. Anyone who would assist in burying this ugly episode in our own history should have little to say about Holocaust deniers.

The hysteria raged on. San Francisco's mayor, Angelo Rossi, once gestured to a crowd with his hand and was accused of giving them a "fascist salute." Many an Italian in this country was incarcerated for "sedition and conspiracy". Opera singers were even "locked up". Since a large portion of opera is written in Italian, one could speculate that this was done in another attempt to "silence the enemy's tongue".

Again, I am not insensitive to the treatment of Japanese-Americans in this country during WWII. Their story should be told and their plight remembered. Quite simply, however, ours should also. It is odd that the heartfelt monument I mentioned earlier is built on Ellis Island. (Not because it honors the Japanese victims, but because it excludes the Italian victims). The fact is that the majority the Japanese immigrants of the time were naturalized on Angel Island, which is in San Francisco Bay. Obviously, millions of Italians entered the continent through Ellis Island. Although I do think that Angel Island is a more appropriate place for a monument to past generations of Japanese Americans, I do not object to the existence of the display on Ellis Island. I object to the omission of the Italian-American from the tribute. It seems that once again, insult is added to injury in the name of "political correctness". The victims of these oppressions are gone now, but their sons and daughters are fighting to tell their stories. Here again, the mainstream media is largely indifferent to their struggle.

It would not be fitting to close the topic of Italians during WWII without taking a look at Mussolini. There is, at this time, a substantial effort underway by quite a few prestigious historians, both Italian and non-Italian to redeem the name of Benito Mussolini for posterity. One key argument in the effort is that after witnessing the fall of Poland and other European countries at the hands of the Nazis, Mussolini joined hands with Hitler in a desperate attempt to soften the blows that the war would inflict on his nation. The geography of Italy itself supports this hypothesis. By simply looking at a map of the European continent, one can clearly see the boot-shaped peninsula precariously dangling almost directly under the powerful Germany of "Der Fuhrer".

Personally, I am undecided as to whether or not I back the movement to "wash clean" the memory of the Italian dictator. However, there are a couple of factors you should take into account while pondering your own position on the issue. First of all, unlike Hitler and the Japanese leaders of the time, Mussolini neither perpetrated nor did he endorse any acts or policies which would have led to genocide. Statistics support this statement. In fact, at the beginning of the war, while he was in power, Jews from other parts of Europe would try to make it to Italy, because they knew they would be safe there.

At the end of the war, most European countries had lost 85% of their Jewish populations. Italy, on the other hand, had lost 65%. This is partially because Italian citizens did a superb job of hiding their Jewish countrymen, after the German invasion. (At the beginning of the war when Mussolini was in power, there was no need for them to hide). Contrary to popular propaganda, the church was instrumental in supporting Jews and other targeted people in hiding. Italy had a sophisticated black market in place which was used to feed and provide for such people. Most informed people know that it was not only Jews that were slaughtered by Hitler, but also Gypsies, Poles, and disabled people were among the victims. What many are not aware of, however, is that devout Catholics were targeted and executed, as well. Hitler knew that their position on the sanctity of human life would cause him opposition. Among the victims of the holocaust were 4,500 Catholic priests, mostly from Italy, who were killed in the concentration camps because they would not cooperate with the Nazis.

Before the war, Mussolini was known for increasing rights for the common people. In the 1930's, in some rural parts of the country, the throwback to the manor system was uncanny. Mussolini is credited for improving the working conditions for the country's agrarian laborer. He also increased public education in Italy and is most famous for extending it to girls. There is no doubt that if he led the nation in the absence of a great world war, history would have treated him much differently.

As fate would have it, Italy did end up fighting a great and costly war. In the collective consciousness here on the home front, the boot shaped nation was grouped in with the Axis Powers or "The Big Three". The mother country was "swept up" and "lumped in" with Germany and Japan as one of the great oppressors. Now, there was a war going on and political cartoons were deemed essential. Cartoons which portrayed German, Japanese and Italian soldiers were commonplace within many publications. But even here in the realm of satire, the treatment of the three groups of men was different. German and Japanese soldiers were depicted as cruel, evil and vindictive. Yet, they were also portrayed as cunning, cleaver and calculating. They were presented as bad, but never as stupid. The Italian soldier was shown in an entirely different light. He was allotted all of the negative traits above, but he was also a "dummy". By all firsthand accounts, the actual Italian soldier in WWII fought with a shrewd valor and was usually outnumbered and using outdated weapons. Yet, the stateside "yellow" press reinvented him with a series of idiotic antics, such as holding his rifle backwards and aiming it at himself. I do understand that, until very recently, war publications were not expected to be politically correct. Still, I certainly would not be sighting this as an injustice if the same moronic traits had been thrust upon the German and Japanese caricatures. Perhaps, stateside papers were already so accustomed to drawing Italian-Americans as imbeciles that at least some of these cartoons were the results of the force of habit.

If you remember one thing about WWII as an Italian-American, it should be that more of us fought and died in this war than did any other ethnicity! I cannot repeat this enough. This fact alone should silence the fools who say we are not behaving enough like Americans. There are too many fascinating tales of these home-grown, polenta-fed heroes to summarize. There are also millions upon millions of Italian-Americans who picked up the torch on the home front and helped lead the nation to victory. Once again, those who are remembered for their honorable acts are often not remembered for their ethnicity.

Rose Bonavita, for example, an Italian-American woman living in Long Island, was the authentic "Rosie the Riveter." When Rose Bonavita's husband went off to war, she picked up his lunch box and went to work in a factory which made fighter planes. Hollywood released a film entitled "Rosie the Riveter", which starred Janey Frazer as "Rosie Warren". This movie told Bonavita's life story, but only partially. We can plainly see which part was omitted. Unfortunately, the real life "shero", whose husband was overseas fighting for her freedom, had her own identity "whitewashed" away on the silver screen. Given the fact that more Italian-Americans were fighting in the war than were any other ethnicity, I said it again. It would stand to reason that there were probably more "Rosas" and "Rosettas" at home than there were "Rosies". Once again, Hollywood was consistent to its legacy. If the Italian character is not a negative one, they simply erase his or her "Italianness".

After the war, the anglicization of Italian-Americans off screen had picked up steam. For the first time, second generation Italian-Americans outnumbered first generation Italian-Americans. Years of discrimination and conditioning from the popular culture may have played equal parts in this widespread attempt by Italian-Americans to hide, or at least suppress their identities. Although for many decades prior to this, Italians in this country had been amputating the vowels from the ends of their names and changing their customs, styles and behaviors to better fit with those of the host culture, there seemed to be a mass exodus amongst Italian-American youth away from anything xenocentric. This did not, however, curb the prejudice. Those who wished to hold on to their language and to some of the old ways, were now not only pressured by non-Italians to "abandon ship", but often by their own family members. Our native tongue had been suppressed within the mainstream culture for decades. Now, it was being silenced in the home, as well.

There was another threat to the survival of the mother culture in the Italian-American home "brewing on the horizon" simultaneously. Italian neighborhoods began to shrink as crime within large cities increased. Many Italian-American men returning from WWII took advantage of the "G.I. Bill". They attended college, became degreed and bought into the suburban dream. Others did not leave their communities voluntarily.

In my city of Chicago, the Italian neighborhoods did not "die a natural death". They were viciously murdered by the great Chicago political machine which was run by the Irish mafia. In the 1950's and early 1960's, Chicago's first Mayor Richard Daley executed a complex and deliberate plan to destroy the city's "Little Italys." By building expressways through them, erecting low-income housing projects within them and refusing to respond to calls to the police department from them, he substantially shrank the city's Italian communities and population. In the heart of the city's largest Italian neighborhood, which is known simply as, "Taylor Street" the mayor constructed the University of Illinois Chicago campus. This required a tremendous portion of the neighborhood to be torn down. When Rose Scala, a vocal community based Italian-American activist exposed the mayor's plan and intent at a press conference, her house was "mysteriously" burned to the ground. Incidentally, the arson was never investigated by the

Chicago Police Department. A similar plan was implemented in New York shortly after the devastation of the Taylor Street neighborhood which successfully depopulated and more or less "choked and killed" the South Bronx altogether.

As the presence of the Irish mafia in local government was thriving, government at the federal level followed suit. Anyone who knows anything at all about the Kennedy family should know how Joe Kennedy made his fortune and achieved the family's social status. He was a bootlegger. He held a high position in the Irish mob and he used the power it brought him to run illegal alcohol shipments during prohibition. If Joe Kennedy were to compare resumes with Al Capone, they would probably end up interviewing for the same jobs. Yet somehow, Kennedy's son managed to become President of the United States. How far do you think that Al Capone's son, Sonny, would have gotten if he had decided to throw his hat into the ring?

Here in Chicago the natives often say, "Vote early and vote often". I have seen the ballot boxes remain untouched for days and even weeks after elections results have been reported. I have also heard the stories about ballots found floating in the river and busloads of homeless people being escorted into the polls and then handed cash after completing the job. We also all know which Irish politician's district will deliver twenty thousand votes in the eleventh hour of any election and insure that the current "chosen one" will be elected. Hence, I am not entirely convinced that JFK "won" the presidency. I live in Chicago and I have seen how the elections are handled. Electronic voting changes little. I know that it was Illinois and particularly Chicago which delivered Kennedy the crucial votes that would push him over the top in 1960. Yet, in the face of all of this, there is still a widespread blindness to the mere existence of this criminal monster which has afflicted our society so tremendously.

In all seriousness, I am relatively confident in saying Al Capone's son probably would not have been my first choice for the presidency if I had been here to cast my vote, at the time. (Not that my vote would have counted in Chicago). However, Mario Cuomo once implied that he could never make a run for the top office because of some similar family circumstances. This is terribly unfortunate. I am sure whatever his family skeletons may be, his father certainly was not a high-ranking mobster as was Joe Kennedy. If it were the case, you certainly would have heard about it given that Cuomo is Italian. Fiorello LaGuardia's family was as "clean as a whistle" and he was still viciously rejected throughout the southern states as a presidential hopeful, simply because he was Italian. This is truly a shame given that as he spent the bulk of his career aggressively fighting organized crime.

While the Irish mafia was busy infesting America's political systems, the Jewish mafia was enjoying some success in that pursuit also, but was mainly busy becoming a powerful force in taking over the country's entertainment industry. I have read some ridiculous rebuttals written by questionable, or at least hyper-defensive, individuals on this topic. There are those who launch attacks on anyone who suggests that a powerful, brutal and influential Jewish mafia exists are being "anti-Semitic". I will not give in to this bullying. The idea that acknowledging that such an organization exists is by some means demeaning to honest law-abiding Jewish people is ridiculous. I do not know any Italian-Americans who pretend that the Italian-Mafia does not exist. I do however know of many a film maker who pretends that it's the only one of its kind and that everyone of Italian heritage is somehow connected to it. The Jewish mafia has been every bit as powerful, corrupt and vicious as the Italian and Irish mafias. They have also used their influence in the entertainment industry to create, perpetuate and intensify the slander of Italian-Americans. As far as the overrepresentation of the Italian mafia in film is concerned, I believe the Jewish mafia has strategically used the Italian mob as a "cultural decoy" to their own "outfit".

That being said, from roughly 1920 to 1980, the Jewish mob was the largest and most powerful syndicate in the country. In the 1920's, Hollywood's movie business was in its beginnings. The first "talkie" was not released until 1929. The Jewish mob did not miss the opportunity to sink their teeth into the opportunities that the studios could provide them. They were instrumental in weaving their way into every facet of the industry. They clearly "called the shots" as to the content of the scripts, as well. It seems obvious that the members of a criminal organization would not want to draw attention to themselves. Given that they had the power to have themselves either written in or out of a story, they took advantage of the situation. Consequently, the existence of the Jewish mafia was completely ignored by the filmmakers of the era, (and every other era, for that matter).

Likewise, the Irish mafia had been written out of existence by the politically motivated print-based media. Meanwhile, on the silver screen, the Jewish Mafioso never made an appearance. In order to fill the suspicious void, both media grossly amplified the existence of the Italian mafia.

It is clearly visible that the entertainment industry has neither subsided in its overrepresentation of Italian-Americans as "Mafioso", nor any other stereotype, over time. The foul practice of disregarding the existence of organized crime rings composed of other ethnicities has also "picked up steam", over time.

The best example of this practice is put into play into what is considered a "classic" mob movie, though I cringe at this term. The character "The Godfather" was actually based on Meyer Lansky. Lansky was a Jewish Mafioso who was very influential in the construction of Las Vegas and in the booming growth of Hollywood. He is said to have been far meaner and more vicious than Capone. And reportedly, he did not hold himself to the same code of chivalry. Unlike Capone, Lansky was not above using women and children as targets for retaliation.

This is truly a painful irony because this, to my knowledge, is the only case of a major production turning Jewish characters into Italian characters. It saddens me that it was Mario Puzo, an Italian-American who wrote the script and that so many of the most prestigious Italian-American actors of the time appeared in the film. It seems that Puzo understood to whom he was selling the book and later the script and was willing to rewrite history, or at least deny it in order to make a sale. We can certainly be our own worst enemies.

When I elaborate upon the various mafias and their areas of "specialization", keep in mind that I am generalizing. Every mafia: Irish, Jewish, Italian, Chinese, Portuguese, Russian, etc., have also been involved in drug running, prostitution, and almost any other illegal and exploitive activity one can fathom. There is also a large amount of fluidity and overlap within these crime rings in and out of the "specialty zones". Still, each crime ring does seem to dominate certain areas of the criminal empire.

The Italian mafia, in addition to engaging in the garden variety of racketeering, successfully drove its stakes into the nation's labor unions in their early stages. Before looking at this any further, we should really have a clear understanding of the history of unions in America. Many people today do not and this is putting us in a very precarious position as a nation and as a people. I am now referring to all Americans.

At the turn of the last century, the working conditions for the laborers in this country were deplorable. Sixteen to eighteen hour days were common. Mills, factories, mines and farms were dangerous and often debilitating, if not deadly. Workers were often killed or maimed in accidents on the worksite, and there was also certainly no public aid or workman's compensation to compensate or feed the starving invalid or his family members. Workers were locked into large rooms which could reach 120°, in the summers. In the winter, they froze. They were often physically abused by the foremen. They labored slavishly for poverty level wages. They lost fingers in machinery, were crushed and suffocated in coal mining accidents and died young of "brown lung disease" from working in the textile mills.

One of the most heinous events of the pre-union era is now known as the "triangle fire". In a New York City textile plant in Lower Manhattan, dozens of young women and girls were either burned to death or jumped out of windows fleeing the flames, only to die on impact. These girls, who were largely Italian, were working up to eighteen hours a day as seamstresses and carrying their sewing machines home each night on their backs. One day as the young women labored away, the building caught fire and soon began to burn out of control. They tried to escape, only to learn that they had been locked in the room. The owner later reported that it was common practice to lock the doors to prevent the employees from "wasting time" in the bathroom.

At this place and time the "American Dream" was looking more like a nightmare to the working class. This was probably the case for many an Italian in the states. The agrarian way of life was dwindling, and all of the farmland was spoken for. If you were a laborer, no matter how hard-working you were, you stood very little chance of rising above your class. More likely than not, your children would have to leave school early to take a menial job, as well. You could, most likely, not earn enough money to support them and your very human body would not be able to withstand the torture of your workplace until a "ripe old age".

Thus, the cycle of poverty was in place. The "throwback" to the European manner system which Caucasian-Americans came to our shores trying to escape was uncanny. The handful of entrepreneurs who "made it to the top", were ruthlessly sucking the life's blood out of the unfortunate masses so that they could continue to amass more and more wealth. The only way to topple this empirical cycle was to unionize labor in America.

This is not a book about the history of organized labor in America, although I know many people today who need to read one. I will not go into great detail about the harsh and bloody battles our forefathers fought in forming unions and achieving decent working conditions. Many of them were abused at work and fired, for the cause. Some were beaten, starved while striking, and even murdered. (Remember, the "aristocracy" never parts with its assets peacefully). Yet, through many years of blood, sweat, tears and sacrifice, unions were formed and strengthened and gained rights for their workers.

The causes of the unions were just and noble. Child labor laws were amongst the first victories the unions enjoyed. The Hay Market Riots ushered in the implementation of the forty hour work week and workman's compensation laws were soon passed to assist those who had been seriously injured on the job. Employers were pressured to improve safety conditions in the workplace and minimum wage laws were passed. Once again, there was hope for the future and people dreamed of a better way of life for their children, who incidentally began to remain in school longer.

Whether or not you like hearing this, unions built the middle class in this country. The popularity of "union bashing" at our present point in history terrifies me. George Santayana once said, "Those who do not study the lessons of history are doomed to repeat them". I do not want to repeat the "Dark Ages" of the American worker. I am the first to admit that unions went too far, particularly in the sixties, seventies and eighties, and ran amuck with corruption. This occurred at the hands of the Italian mafia, particularly our homegrown "La Cosa Nostra". I also agree that unions need to be cleaned up. Yet, we cannot afford to throw away the baby with the bathwater, particularly when "the baby" is the American Dream.

I want gangsters tried and sentenced. I want unions "cleaned up." However, I do not believe that it is the presence of the mafia within the unions which has the "feds" all over them. I think it is the presence of the Italian mafia which has brought on this response. Whenever there is a "crackdown" on organized crime, it always seems to be within the labor unions. Could it be that someone else wants to stick some fingers into this pie? I would like to see some investigations underway involving mob activity in local government and in the entertainment industry. I encourage you to do a little of your own research into the crimes of the Jewish and Irish and other ethnic mafias.

GIVEN OUR HISTORY, IT SHOULD NOT COME AS ANY SURPRISE THAT MANY ACCOMPLISHMENTS MADE BY ITALIANS AND ITALIAN AMERICANS HAVE EITHER GONE UNRECOGNIZED OR HAVE BEEN ACCREDITED TO NON-ITALIANS.

A quarter of a century before Marconi "made waves" with his invention of the radio in the motherland, the ingenious breakthrough of another Italian scientist was heisted and became synonymous with the name of its thief himself. On that note, it is now officially documented by the U.S. government that the telephone was not actually invented by Scottish-American, Alexander Graham Bell, but by an Italian immigrant by the name of Antonio Meucci. It is, in fact, so well documented that Congress issued an official statement in 2002 stating that Meucci was the true inventor. Meucci lost out on the paycheck, because he could not afford a patent.

Patent problems seemed to be a plague among early inventors. Likewise, most women's history courses teach that Eli Whitney did not invent the cotton gin. Catherine Green, the actual inventor or the cotton gin was the wife of Nathaniel Green. It is said that a woman could not legally obtain a patent in the 1800's, so Whitney slyly "jumped in" and took advantage of the situation. At any rate, patent corruption was rampant, and Italians in this country were often poor.

In other cases the denial of our accomplishment is more subtle. At times when the Italian's great feat is not possible to ignore, a non-Italian is frequently pushed into the spotlight to upstage him/her. There is a "tale of two geniuses" that tells this story eloquently. Their names are Albert Einstein and Enrico Fermi.

Both of these men were racking up numerous accomplishments prior to the Manhattan Project. They both were Nobel Prize winners. Einstein is remembered primarily for his theory of relativity and Fermi for building the first functioning nuclear reactor. They also both fled Europe because of Hitler's policies, particularly toward the Jews. (Fermi's wife was Jewish).

Amongst physicists, Enrico Fermi is considered to have been the greatest intellect of all time. Yet, he is all but forgotten by the mainstream culture, whereas Albert Einstein has become synonymous with "genius". His picture appears on posters which read, "Think for Yourself". I can remember a time in which the phrase, "He's no Einstein", was a popular way of saying someone was dimwitted. I never, on the other hand heard anyone say, "He's no Fermi." Why could the Italian genius not be given the job as the "poster child?" Think about who might have made this choice. History has certainly had its share of brilliant Italians. Cicero, da Vinci, Michelangelo, Galileo, Marconi, Meucci, Dante are just the tip of the iceberg.

I have given the Einstein v. Fermi issue a lot of consideration. At one point, I thought that Einstein was the "chosen one" because he was a colorful character. The wild hair and the stories of him wearing mismatched socks may be endearing. Then, I learned that Enrico Fermi was perhaps not as eccentric as Einstein, but every bit as unique. What set Enrico Fermi apart from other men of his caliber was his kindness and simplicity. It was not unusual to spot the great scientist taking out the garbage in his lab or eating lunch with the janitor. One visitor to his lab once marveled to see him moving a table with a graduate student under the direction of another graduate student. It appears that Fermi not only possessed exceptional intellect, but exceptional kindness and humility, as well.

As Enrico Fermi and Albert Einstein were intellectual giants, Mother Cabrini and Mother Theresa of Calcutta were humanitarian giants. For the record: Mother Theresa was Yugoslavian and Mother Cabrini was Italian. Both of these selfless women accomplished milestones far beyond what most people even hoped for in either time. Most relatively well-informed people are at least somewhat aware of the amazing acts of charity performed by Mother Theresa. Though sadly, many are completely uninformed as to those of Mother Cabrini, who was very much the "Mother Theresa" of her time. The strength, faith, compassion and fortitude of both of these women is awe inspiring and I am confident in saying they each left the world a better place. Yet, it is only Mother Theresa who is remembered as the pinnacle of virtue and altruism. As Einstein and Fermi were, more or less, "identical geniuses", I dare say that Mother Theresa and Mother Cabrini were "identical humanitarians".

Francesca Cabrini was born in 1850 and died in 1917. She was originally from Italy and wanted to travel to China to serve and evangelize. Instead of Asia, the pope sent Francesca to New York to help ease the suffering of Italians in the United States. In short, Mother Cabrini founded sixty-seven institutions worldwide. She founded and ran orphanages, schools, hospitals, nurseries and homes for those who had none. These establishments were located in North and South America, throughout Europe, (including Siberia), and in Asia, (including China).

In short, Mother Cabrini's presence and influence was far more pronounced in America than was Mother Theresa's. Her accomplishments abroad helped pave the way for the path that Mother Theresa would take more than half a century later. Although she helped anyone and everyone who needed assistance, she was particularly instrumental in bringing relief to the most desperate Italians in America. Perhaps this is why the "unenlightened masses" are so disinterested in her beautiful story.

My favorite case of "cultural hijacking" is a full blown identity theft. Before going into this legacy of misperception, I would like to compare two Saint's Days in detail. One is primarily celebrated by the Irish and the other is mainly celebrated by Italians.

The Saint Joseph's Day table originated in Sicily. Centuries ago, there was a famine in the region and the people prayed to Saint Joseph for intercessory prayer. (Contradictory to protestant myth, Catholics do not believe that saints have any power independent from God. They are simply intercessors who can pray for them as could a friend or a neighbor). When the famine ended, the people gave a feast in thanksgiving to God. In gratitude to Saint Joseph, it was named for him and celebrated on his feast day. It was, like most "festas" celebrated in the town's squares and tables were erected with as elaborate a spread as each community could afford. The "Saint Joseph's Day Table", became an annual affair and an act of charity. The poor were served and ate first. This was the one day a year they were able to feast to their hearts' content and were treated like nobility. Unfortunately, in America where main arteries are closed off and rivers are dyed green for Saint Patrick's Day celebrations, the Saint Joseph's Day table is only erected inside church basements and private banquet halls. The thought of giving this warm tradition a public forum does not seem to be of interest, at least within my local government.

As we, this time with our Saint Joseph's Day Tables, managed to end up in the church basements again, two days earlier, the Saint Patrick's Day celebrants guzzle green beer inside, outside and any other place they can find. What they often do not realize is that instead of green beer, they should really be drinking red wine. Saint Patrick, the patron saint of Ireland was actually a Roman. That would, for all practical purposes, make him-yes, Italian!

Saint Patrick's birth name was Patricius Julius; this sounds as Roman as "Caesar" to me. We all remember Julius Caesar from history class. Perhaps, you also remember that the "Patricians" were the ruling class of Ancient Rome. I probably could not find a more Roman name if I tried. He was the son of a high ranking official in the Roman government named Calphurnius and his wife Conchessa. These names are still sounding really Roman. His birthplace was Dumbarton, Scotland and he lived there from 387 to 493 AD. During this period, the Romans still occupied the majority of the British Isles. The reason for my precision in this description is deliberate. I have argued with many a Shamrock-waving celebrant on March 17th as to Saint Patrick's origins. Needless to say, they do not always welcome my history lesson with open arms. Make no mistake and if in doubt, do your own research. The Romans kept fastidious records and so did the church. Saint Patrick was, beyond a shadow of a doubt, a Roman.

As the rest of the story goes, at age sixteen, Julius Patricius was kidnapped by Celtic marauders, taken to Ireland and sold into slavery. For six years, he labored under the whip of a cruel master. During this time, he prayed fervently for his comfort and freedom. He was, by all accounts, at least a third generation Christian. He also became fluent in the Celtic tongue. At the end of six years, Patricius escaped, unharnessed a boat from a nearby harbor and sailed to England.

By this time, he had decided to give his life to the service of God. He entered a seminary where he studied and became a priest. At his own request, he returned to Ireland where he evangelized, served the poor and lead an exemplary life. He died on March 17th, 493 at the age of one hundred five.

So, Patricius served Christianity throughout Ireland. Given that he returned so many decades of altruistic service to the country that stole his youth and tried to work him to death, they could not have found a finer person to choose as their patron saint. Yet, he was not, by any stretch of the imagination, Irish.

As Saint Patrick's Day is celebrated on the public spectrum with parades, environmental damage to waterways, foul displays of public drunkenness, etc., it is sad to say that this fine man's memory is reduced to such "shenanigans". If this is the way the Saint Joseph's Day Table would be treated on the outside, I would prefer to remain in the church basement.

As I have pondered the ingredients of this "perfect storm" we have been caught in from my church basement, I have come to the conclusion that one of the top "culture killers" for those of us of Italian heritage in North America is who we have "melted into the pot" with. In elaboration, many Italians also immigrated to South America. On that continent, however, interracial marriages have been more common than they have been in North America. Many South American families have children of various pigments and features because, in many countries, it is not unusual for them to have Indian, African and European ancestry within the same family. Until very recently, in North America, this was far more uncommon.

Although Italians were not viewed as "White" in many parts of the United States, in the cities of the north, interethnic marriages started becoming commonplace, particularly after WWII. Italians married Anglo-Saxons frequently. This diluted our heritage, because we married the "diluters" themselves. The "speak only English" people became the parents of our children. Being half Italian meant that you, more than likely, had one parent that was very well versed in the host culture and thought that it was the only one you needed to understand in order to prosper in this country. That parent, more than likely, discouraged the speaking of Italian by the children, thinking he or she was acting in their best interest. Since Italians are, in fact, Caucasian, it was possible to douse the unwanted traits with a coat of white paint.

You cannot put one coat of white paint over a black wall or a dark brown wall and make it look white. Yet, you can make a beige or a cream colored wall look white with only one coat of white paint. As you know, the paint must be placed in the superior position for this to occur. In this country, when the Italian beige was mixed with the Anglo-Saxon white, the white coat was always in the superior position. All of the necessary primers had been applied for this phenomenon to be inevitable. Therefore, the "paper covers rock" syndrome, generally, choked the Italian heritage right out of the bicultural child, or at least senselessly diluted it. Getting it back years later will require diligent effort.

Any American searching for their English, Irish, Welsh, or Scottish heritage will be able to acquire it almost effortlessly. After all, we live in an English speaking country which sprang forth from a group of English colonies and was designed by our founding fathers who were not entirely, but overwhelmingly, English. I would go so far as to say that people of this heritage, or partially of this heritage, could not completely disconnect with their heritage while living in this country, even if they tried.

As presented earlier, the connection between language and culture alone is so primal that where language prevails, culture prevails. Dialects reflect and change culture, as well. Henceforth, unless your primary language of heredity is Spanish or English, you will need to put forth some effort to maintain the culture of your forefathers, while living in this country. As an Italian, the language connection may be more challenging for you than to members of some other ethnic groups who did not have theirs forcibly taken from them.

The question of who we are as Italian-Americans cannot be answered in a paragraph. As our culture has been distorted, diluted, dismissed and ridiculed by many others on this continent, some of us have backed away from it and become embarrassed by and ashamed of our roots. Many a paisano in America has internalized the ugly message that in order to be accepted, we must change the fabric of who we are. Yet, in many of us, the persecution only deepens our yearning for our culture and for a connection to the motherland. It is a healthy pursuit for Italian-Americans to study the language, deepen our understanding of the culture, travel to Italy and join Italian-American societies. I encourage all of these very healthy and enlightening endeavors.

Please, remember as you proceed, you are not only Italian, you are also Italian-American. You need to know your Italian history, but not at the expense of your American or your Italian-American history. You are unmistakably Italian and also a full-blooded American whose family, most likely, lost at least one member fighting in a war defending the red, white and blue.

Italian history has been anything but a "cake walk" for millennia. Yet, our experiences are not the same. In Italy, Italians are the mainstream culture. They do not have to fight to be recognized as dignified or intelligent. Any public ridicule of their ways is merely a matter of "poking fun at oneself" and no one is ever told not to speak, act or be Italian. The bountiful accomplishments within their legacy are celebrated and never denied, as they are here. Clearly, they have seen dramatic tragedies and struggles throughout their heritage which have not been less than our own. They have, however, been different.

Modern Italians living on "the boot" are very different from our nonni and bisnonni. If you have traveled to Italy, I am sure you will agree that our grandparents and great-grandparents presented a much different image than today's tres chic, high fashion, fast-driving Italian.

We understand that America has changed drastically since our forefathers arrived on its shores. Make no mistake that Italy has changed, as well. Though many attributes of the culture have withstood the test of time, many more have not. The end result is that, in many ways, we have a cultural identity that is more closely tied to Italians of the past than those of the present. There is, however, nothing wrong with this. Linguists agree that the English being spoken in Appalachia today is closer to the English of William Shakespeare than that which is now spoken in London. This is, of course, because, of the near isolation of this English-speaking population for over two centuries. Yet, no one would disagree that the Appalachian Americans of today are very different than the modern Scots and Brits.

As stated, as the plight of our image is a phenomenon caused by any number of factors working together; your actual self-image should also be based upon a multitude of factors. Please embrace the culture of YOUR ancestors and understand the two or more countries that breathed life into you. It is impossible to understand who you are, if you do not truly understand who they were. Your nonni and bisnonni were the Italians of a different generation. They left Italy in search of a better way of life for themselves and their offspring and that includes you. Understand their struggle and learn as much about them as possible; do not omit their language. In learning the language which was extracted from our mouths and exploring the culture you will encounter self-truths beyond your wildest imagination.

Whether or not you are a "history buff", you should know the basics of Italian history and American history and have a particular understanding of Italian-American history because you are living it. I will not continue with a "laundry list" on how to explore your own identity because it is your identity, hence an individual process and decision. However, as one Italian-American to another, I must say that we all need to inventory our self-perceptions regularly as a form of "damage control", given the harsh climate in which these perceptions exist. We cannot take for granted that we know who we are in the environment in which we live. We have had too many sources telling us that we are something else.

Above all else, please, do not ignore ugliness when it is "thrust in your face". Confront the mud slinger. Do not use the excuse that you are non-combative or simply not confrontational. Non-confrontational people NEVER stop injustice. Speak up! Tell the offenders what you think of their stupid jokes. Write the networks and tell them what you think of their offensive scripts. Don't just sit there and take it; do something about it! Your forefathers and foremothers endured the sweat shops, lynchings, deculturalization, insults, exclusions, and any other number of agonies for you to have a "better way of life". If we would band together and fight one tenth as hard as they did, we could swiftly stop our cultural persecutors. Once again: Most Italian-Americans believe that when they voice their point of view to non-Italians, they do not listen. The bigger problem seems to be that Italian-Americans of our generation will not talk. SPEAK UP!

Bibliography

www.biography.com/people/enricofermie9293405

http://whereitgoesin.blogspot.com/2005/10/
defending-Mussolinis-bad-namehtml

http:/hipsterjew.com2010/03/22jewish-mafia-movies

http://www.publicbookshelf.com/public-html/OurCountry-Vol-1/
whoisherbj.html

http://www.theholedayspot.com/patrick/historyofpatrick.stm

http://www.pathos.com/Resources/Additional-Resources/
From-Columbus-to-Cabrini-Am

www.theguardian.com/Humanities

www.theAtlantic.com/1927/sacco-and-vanzetti/306625/

www.history.com/thisdayin./sacco-and-vanzetti-executed

www.readperiodicals.com>2004/09/rosieriveter-Italian.html.

https/www.washingtonpost/.rosiethe-riveter

www.islandlowblog.com/
filippo-mazzei-and-the-declaration-of-independence

www.Fra Noi

http://at j g 64:tripod.com/italianharlem.html

http://www.care2.com/c2c/groups/disc.
html?gpp=6454&pst=274751

bioguidebritannica.com//Fiorello-H-La-Guardia

Https://msu.edu/-szandzi2/alcaponelegacy.html